AUG 1 4 2007

T3-BHM-444

612.17 KIN

My Body

My Heart

WITHDRAWN

by
Carol K.
Lindeen

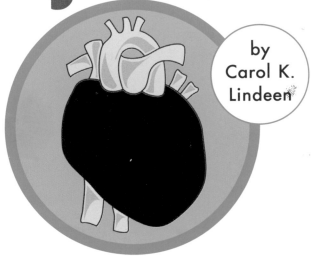

Consulting Editor: Gail Saunders-Smith, PhD

Consultant: James R. Hubbard, MD
Fellow in the American Academy of Pediatrics
Iowa Medical Society, West Des Moines, Iowa

Capstone
press

Mankato, Minnesota

Bloomingdale
Public Library
101 Fairfield Way
Bloomingdale, IL 60108

Pebble Books are published by Capstone Press,
151 Good Counsel Drive, P.O. Box 669, Mankato, Minnesota 56002.
www.capstonepress.com

Copyright © 2007 by Capstone Press. All rights reserved.
No part of this publication may be reproduced in whole or in part,
or stored in a retrieval system, or transmitted in any form or by any means,
electronic, mechanical, photocopying, recording, or otherwise,
without written permission of the publisher.
For information regarding permission, write to Capstone Press,
151 Good Counsel Drive, P.O. Box 669, Dept. R, Mankato, Minnesota 56002.
Printed in the United States of America

1 2 3 4 5 6 12 11 10 09 08 07

Library of Congress Cataloging-in-Publication Data
Lindeen, Carol, 1976–
    My heart / by Carol K. Lindeen.
    p. cm.—(Pebble Books. My body)
    Summary: "Simple text and photographs describe the heart and how it
works"—Provided by publisher.
    Includes bibliographical references and index.
    ISBN-13: 978-0-7368-6691-0 (hardcover)
    ISBN-10: 0-7368-6691-4 (hardcover)
    ISBN-13: 978-0-7368-7835-7 (softcover pbk.)
    ISBN-10: 0-7368-7835-1 (softcover pbk.)
    1. Heart—Juvenile literature. I. Title.
QP111.6.L56 2007
612.1'7—dc22   2006013650

Note to Parents and Teachers

The My Body set supports national science standards related to anatomy and the basic structure and function of the human body. This book describes and illustrates the heart. The photographs support early readers in understanding the text. The repetition of words and phrases helps early readers learn new words. This book also introduces early readers to subject-specific vocabulary words, which are defined in the Glossary section. Early readers may need assistance to read some words and to use the Table of Contents, Glossary, Read More, Internet Sites, and Index sections of the book.

Table of Contents

My Heartbeat

Thump, thump.

Thump, thump.

I can feel my heart

beat inside my chest.

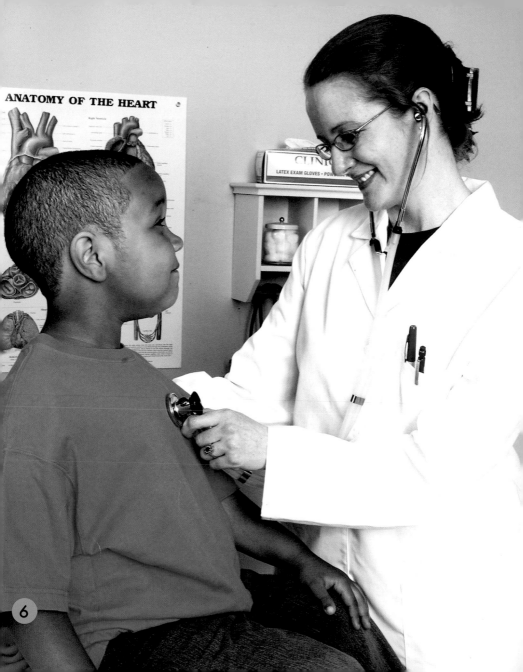

My heart makes a
soft sound when it beats.
My heart pumps blood
through my body.

I feel a little beat
in my wrist. It's my pulse.
My pulse tells me
my heart is working.

On the Inside

My heart is
a strong muscle
in my chest.

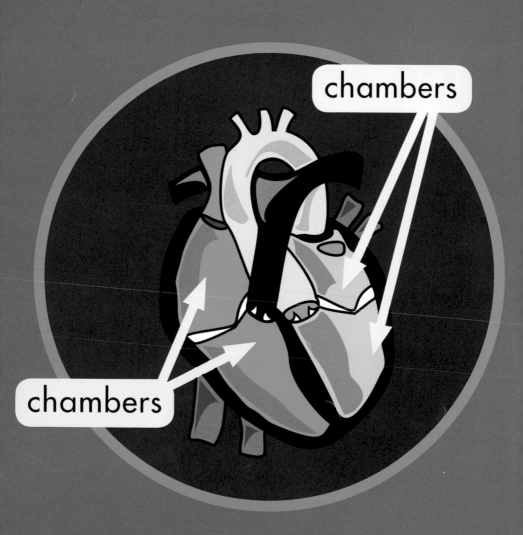

My heart has four spaces called chambers.
Blood moves in and out of the chambers.

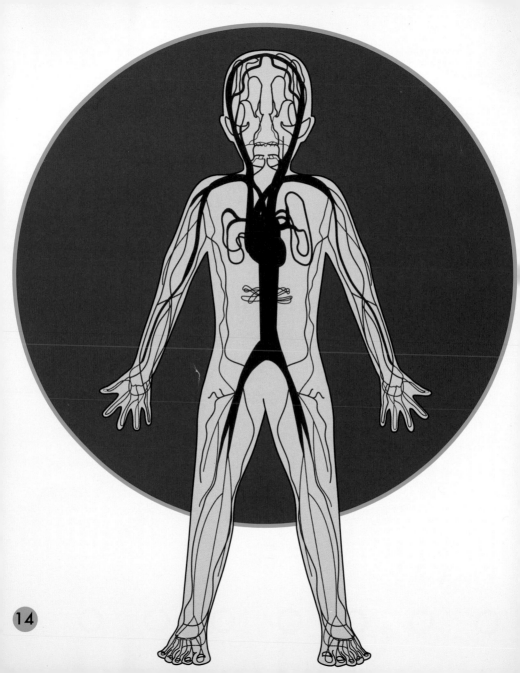

My Heart and My Body

Blood vessels carry blood to and from my heart.

Blood vessels take blood to my fingers and toes. My brain and stomach need blood, too.

My heart pumps slower
when I sleep.
It pumps faster
when I run.

My lungs and heart
keep my blood pumping.
My heart keeps
my whole body healthy.

Glossary

blood vessel—a narrow tube that carries blood through your body

chamber—an enclosed space; a person's heart has four chambers.

flow—to move along smoothly

pulse—a steady beat or throb; your pulse is the beating of major blood vessels as your heart pumps; you can feel your pulse in your wrist and neck.

pump—to force or push something; the heart pumps blood through the body by squeezing; this pushes blood through the blood vessels.

Read More

Curry, Don L. *How Does Your Heart Work?* Rookie Read-about Health. New York: Children's Press, 2003.

Nettleton, Pamela Hill. *Thump-Thump: Learning About Your Heart.* The Amazing Body. Minneapolis: Picture Window Books, 2004.

Internet Sites

FactHound offers a safe, fun way to find Internet sites related to this book. All of the sites on FactHound have been researched by our staff.

Here's how:

1. Visit *www.facthound.com*
2. Choose your grade level.
3. Type in this book ID **0736866914** for age-appropriate sites. You may also browse subjects by clicking on letters, or by clicking on pictures and words.
4. Click on the **Fetch It** button.

FactHound will fetch the best sites for you!

Index

Word Count: 125
Grade: 1
Early-Intervention Level: 15

Editorial Credits
Mari Schuh, editor; Bobbi J. Wyss, designer; Sandy D'Antonio, illustrator;
    Kelly Garvin, photo stylist

Photo Credits
Capstone Press/Karon Dubke, all

3 1531 00318 0855